LEVEL
2
AGES 7 AND 8

TROPICAL RAIN FOREST

April Pulley Sayre

SCHOLASTIC
REFERENCE

PHOTO CREDITS: Cover: Stephen Dalton/Photo Researchers, Inc. Page 1: April Pulley Sayre; 3: Jacques Jangoux/Photo Researchers, Inc.; 4: © Royalty Free/Corbis; 5: Aaron Haupt/Photo Researchers, Inc.; 7: Tom & Pat Leeson/Photo Researchers, Inc.; 8: Wayne Lawler/ Photo Researchers, Inc.; 9: April Pulley Sayre; 10: Luiz C. Marigo/Peter Arnold, Inc.; 11: Gregory G. Dimijian/Photo Researchers, Inc.; 12: April Pulley Sayre; 13: Michael Fogden/Bruce Coleman Inc.; 15: Tom & Pat Leeson/Photo Researchers, Inc.; 16: Michael Fogden/Bruce Coleman Inc.; 17: Farrell Grehan/Photo Researchers, Inc.; 18: April Pulley Sayre; 19: Carolyn Iverson/Photo Researchers, Inc.; 21: Norman Owen Tomalin/Bruce Coleman Inc.; 23: Bob Burch/Bruce Coleman Inc.; 24: Michael Fogden/Bruce Coleman Inc.; 25: Fletcher & Baylis/Photo Researchers, Inc.; 27: Michael Fogden/Bruce Coleman Inc.; 28: David M. Schleser/Nature's Images, Inc./Photo Researchers, Inc.; 29: Michael Fogden/Bruce Coleman Inc.; 30: Tim Davis/Photo Researchers, Inc.; 31 (top): Ray Coleman/Photo Researchers, Inc.; 31 (bottom): David M. Schleser/Nature's Images, Inc./ Photo Researchers, Inc.; 32: James H. Carmichael/Photo Researchers, Inc.; 33: Gregory G. Dimijian/Photo Researchers, Inc.; 34; Michael Fogden/Bruce Coleman Inc.; 35: Ivan Polunin/Bruce Coleman Inc.; 36: Leonide Principe/Photo Researchers, Inc.; 37: April Pulley Sayre; 38: Wesley Bocxe/Photo Researchers, Inc.; 39: Karl Weidmann/ Photo Researchers, Inc.; 40: Erwin & Peggy Bauer/Bruce Coleman Inc.; 41: © 318; Gallo Images/Corbis; 43: Michael J. Doolittle/Peter Arnold, Inc.; 45: Kenneth W. Fink/Photo Researchers, Inc.

The animal shown on the title page is a howler monkey.

Library of Congress Cataloging-in-Publication Data available.

ISBN 0-439-35523-0

Book design by Barbara Balch and Kay Petronio
Photo research by Sarah Longacre

10 9 8 7 6 5   05 06

Printed in the U.S.A.   23

First trade printing, March 2003

We are grateful to Francie Alexander, reading specialist, and to Adele M. Brodkin, Ph.D., developmental psychologist, for their contributions to the development of this series.

Our thanks also to our science consultants Dr. Nora Bynum of the Organization for Tropical Studies, and Mark Halvorsen, Tropics Zone Keeper at New York City's Central Park Wildlife Center.

Compared to a city, a tropical rain forest is quiet. Tall trees tower over you, making you feel small. But if you listen carefully, you can hear animals. Frogs chirp. Parrots screech. Insects click. A piece of bark falls. You look up at a tree that is taller than a ten-story building. Howler monkeys hoot and roar.

Tropical rain forests are a special kind of forest. They only grow in the tropics. The tropics is the area just north and south of the equator. The equator is an imaginary line. Like a belt, it circles Earth's middle.

equator

Earth's largest patches of tropical rain forest are in Brazil, Zaire, and Indonesia. Tropical rain forests also grow in other places. They grow in Mexico. They grow in Central America. Tropical rain forests cover parts of islands such as Hawaii, Puerto Rico, and Madagascar.

Tropical rain forests contain many **species**, or kinds, of animals. They have more animal species than other places on Earth. In a rain forest, expert birdwatchers can find 300 bird species in a day. That's more than they may see in a year elsewhere.

In Peru, a scientist found forty-three different ant species on one single tree. That tree had more ant species than the entire country of Finland! Tropical rain forests have so many species that many have not been studied yet. Every year, scientists find new plants and animals in rain forests.

This rain forest bird is a toucan.

*Rain forest leaves often have curved tips,
to help water run off them.*

Rain forest animals must live with rain. Most tropical rain forests receive more than 80 inches (200 centimeters) of rain a year. The air is moist, like air inside a shower stall. But it doesn't rain all the time. It often rains for an hour or so, then stops. The rain drips off curved leaf tips.

Tropical rain forests do not have winter, spring, summer, or fall. But some tropical rain forests have rainy seasons and dry seasons. The month when the rainy season begins varies from place to place. It depends on local geography and climate. The rainy season may last for half a year. During the rainy season it rains almost every day—if only for a few hours. It rains hard. Roads become muddy. Rivers may flood.

A frog sits right in the middle of this picture. It is hidden against dried leaves that have fallen to the ground in a rain forest in Panama.

In Brazil's Amazon Rain Forest, rivers flood the forest. The forests are filled with water for up to five months. Fish swim among the trunks of trees. Animals live in the tops of trees until the water level goes down. This kind of flooding does not happen in every rain forest.

Most tropical rain forests have warm weather. Their average air temperature is 75° to 86°F (24° to 30°C). One kind of rain forest, the **cloud forest**, has cooler air. Cloud forests grow high up on mountains. Clouds and mist keep these forests wet. The quetzal (ket-**sahl**), Guatamala's national bird, lives in cloud forests.

Emergent trees poke through the canopy.

A tropical rain forest has many layers. The roof of the forest is the **canopy**. The canopy is made of treetops. Monkeys, squirrels, and slow-moving mammals called sloths live in the canopy. The canopy is sunny. Flowers bloom. Bees buzz. The canopy has more animal activity than any other part of the forest.

A few extremely tall trees stick up above the canopy. These are called **emergent trees**.

Below the canopy is the **understory**. The understory is shadier than the canopy. Woodpeckers tap on tree trunks. Snakes slither. Iguanas, which are huge lizards, lounge on tree branches. Twisted vines hang from trees. A single vine, stretched out, may reach farther than two football fields!

Vines drape down from the canopy.

Below the understory is the forest floor. This area is often quiet. Trees shade it. Jaguars prowl. Wild pigs wander and large, spotted rodents, called pacas (**pak**-uhs), roam. Once in a while, a dead tree falls.

When a tree falls, sunlight shines through the new hole in the canopy. The sunlight reaches the forest floor. Plants sprout and grow. After many years, they fill the gap in the forest. Small patches of rain forest can regrow in this way. But when trees are removed from a large area, the forest trees may not regrow in the open space.

This jaguar was photographed in a rain forest in Central America.

Rain forests have many kinds of plants. If you take a short walk through another kind of forest, you might see twenty species of trees.

But if you take a short walk through a tropical rain forest, you might see two hundred different plant species!

Lots of rain forest trees are draped with **epiphytes** (**ep**-uh-*fites*). Epiphytes are plants that grow on other plants. Some ferns are epiphytes.

Orchids are epiphytes. Orchid
flowers grow in many colors and
shapes. A scientist counted 300
orchids on one rain forest tree!

Another type of epiphyte is the **bromeliad** (broh-**meel**-ee-*ad*). Bromeliads are related to pineapple plants. Some bromeliads have leaves that form a vase in the center of the plant. Rainwater fills the vase. The water helps the plant in case of dry weather. The bromeliad is also a home for tadpoles, frogs, snakes, lizards, crabs, and insects. It is like an aquarium, up in a tree! A bromeliad vase may hold as much as 30 gallons (114 liters) of water.

Epiphytes don't directly harm trees. But wet, heavy epiphytes can weigh down a tree branch. Then the branch may fall.

When a tree has ripe fruit and nuts, animals gather. Toucans fly in. Their big, strong beaks are good for cracking nuts and eating fruit. Monkeys and bats eat fruit, too.

Birds, monkeys, and bats help plant trees. After meals, fruit eaters' droppings are full of fruit seeds. Sometimes these seeds sprout.

Strangler fig seeds sprout in droppings left on tree branches. So, the fig tree begins life on a branch. It sends down roots to the ground. It sends shoots toward the sun.

A strangler fig tree surrounds a hardwood tree in a rain forest in Africa.

Eventually the strangler fig surrounds the tree it grows on. The strangler fig shades the other tree, blocking the sunlight the tree needs for energy. The original tree dies and the strangler fig takes its place.

Many rain forest plants need animals as **pollinators** (**pahl**-uhn-*nay*-tuhrz). Pollinators carry pollen from flower to flower. Bees are pollinators. Bats, moths, flies, and birds are pollinators, too. When a pollinator visits a plant, pollen gets on its body. This pollen rubs off on the next flower it visits.

A bat visits a flower in a cloud forest in Costa Rica, which is part of Central America.

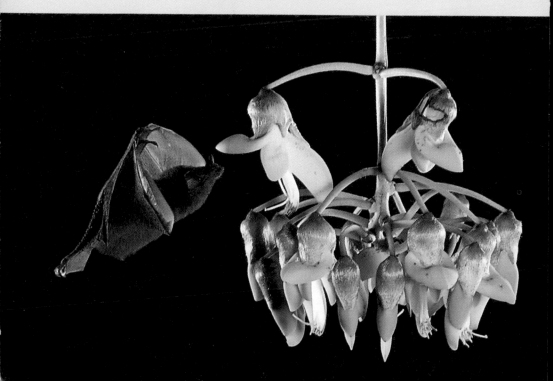

Rafflesia flowers smell terrible to people—but not to flies!

Plants attract pollinators in many different ways. Some make sweet nectar that pollinators can drink. The world's largest flower, the rafflesia (rah-**flee**-zee-uh), attracts pollinators by smelling like rotten meat! This smell attracts flies.

Many rain forest plants and their pollinators fit each other, almost like a hand and a glove. The sword-billed hummingbird has a long bill that fits the passiflora (*pass*-i-**flor**-uh) flower. The sicklebill hummingbird has a curved bill for feeding at the heliconia (*hel*-i-**koe**-nee-uh) plant. The Madagascan hawk moth has an 8-inch- (20-centimeter-) long tongue for feeding at a long-tubed orchid. Many rain forest plants have only one kind of pollinator. These animals help the plants make seeds.

A white-tipped sicklebill feeds at a heliconia flower.

This termite nest is on a tree in Peru's Amazon Rain Forest.

If you like insects, you'll love rain forests. In a rain forest you can see termite and ant nests hanging down from trees. Marching down trees are leaf cutter ants.

They carry leaves and flowers back to their nests. But they don't eat leaves. Leaf cutter ants are fungi (**fuhn**-jye) farmers. Fungi are plant-like organisms such as mushrooms, yeasts, and molds. The ants grow fungi on leaves. Then the ants eat the fungi.

Some rain forest insects are hard to find. They are camouflaged (**kam**-uh-*flahzhed*), meaning they blend in with other things.

Some praying mantises look like green leaves.

Some praying mantises look like dead leaves.

Stick insects look like sticks.

Blue morpho (**more**-foe) butterflies appear bright blue when flying. But when blue morphos land, they close their wings. The outsides of their wings look like dead leaves. So when perched, they are hard to see.

Glass-winged butterflies have clear wings. This is a kind of camouflage, too. Camouflage helps animals hide from other animals that might eat them.

Rain forest trees are full of climbing animals. Monkeys, squirrels, possums, anteaters, and sloths live up in the trees. Sloths move slowly. They eat leaves. Once a week, they climb to the ground, to poop. Then they climb back up their trees.

A three-toed sloth hangs in a tree in Panama, in Central America.

A flying lemur glides through rain forest trees.

To get from tree to tree, some
animals climb. Some jump. Some fly.
Others glide like paper airplanes.
Flying lemurs, flying squirrels, flying
frogs, flying tree snakes, and lizards
called flying dragons glide. Flaps of
skin on their legs, arms, or toes catch
the air like parachutes.

*A young Yanomami boy prepares his bow
for hunting in the rain forest.*

Rain forests contain more than
amazing wild animals and plants. They
are home to many rain forest people.
People such as the Yanomami of Brazil
rely on the forest for shelter and food.

The Yanomami gather leaves, fruits, nuts, and honey from the forest. They hunt animals for meat. They make their homes from rain forest plants.

Like the Yanomami, rain forest people in Central America often use rain forest plants to make their houses.

Unfortunately, rain forests all over the world are in danger. The trees are being cut down. Some are cut for wood to make paper or firewood. Trees are cut down to clear the land. Then the land is used for roads, farms, ranches, or houses.

Often a forest is cleared to create a farm. But the farmer can only grow crops there for a few years. Rain forest soil is not good for farming.

Living forests hold the soil in place. When the trees are logged, the land is left bare.

Rain washes the dirt away.
The dirt clogs rivers. It kills fish.

*Muddy brown water shows that rain forest soil has
washed off this hillside. Once the trees are cut down,
there is nothing to hold the dirt in place.*

It is hard to stop the cutting of the rain forests. Every day, there are more people in the world. People need places for farms and houses. But some people are working to save tropical rain forests. They are asking governments to create parks to protect forests.

Young people, along with a guide, look for canopy birds and animals in a rain forest in Peru.

Meanwhile, somewhere in a rain forest, hummingbirds hover. Pig-like tapirs walk the ground. Butterflies flutter. Tiny monkeys called marmosets snooze. Scientists look in wonder at ants, and plants, and birds. And rain forest people settle down to sleep in their homes.

These small monkeys are marmosets.

Glossary

bromeliad (broh-**meel**-ee-*ad*)—a family of plants. Many bromeliads grow on rain forest trees. Others do not. Spanish moss and pineapple plants are bromeliads.

canopy—the layer formed by the crowns of most rain forest trees

cloud forest—a high mountain rain forest kept wet by clouds

emergent trees—extremely tall trees that stick up above the forest's canopy layer

epiphytes (**ep**-uh-*fites*)—plants that grow perched on other plants

pollinators (**pahl**-uhn-*nay*-tuhrz)—animals or forces that carry pollen from one plant to another

species—a type of animal. Scientists group related organisms into species.

understory—the area beneath a forest's treetops but above the forest floor

Index

A Note to Parents

Learning to read is such an exciting time in a child's life. You may delight in sharing your favorite fairy tales and picture books with your child.

But don't forget the importance of introducing your child to the world of nonfiction. The ability to read and comprehend factual material will be essential to your child in school and throughout life. The Scholastic Science Readers™ series was created especially with beginning readers in mind. These books, with their clear texts and beautiful photographs, will help you to share the wonders of science with *your* new reader.

Suggested Activity

Many plants you see in homes and offices are rain forest plants. That's because plants that grow on the rain forest floor do well in dim light, like that of an office or home. These plants often have large, green, beautiful leaves. Go on a "rain forest hunt," and look for rain forest plants in your home or school. Ask your parent or guardian to help you continue your hunt at an office, mall, florist, or garden center near where you live. Look for orchids, bromeliads, philodendrons, begonias, African violets, and rubber plants. You might find a little bit of the rain forest right in your neighborhood!